Exploring
New Market Street
Usk

Researched and edited by
John F Barrow

Sponsored by Usk Civic Society and
the Roger Edwards Educational Trust

Published by Saron Publishing in 2020

ISBN-13: 978-1-913297-06-0

Saron Publishers
Pwllmeyrick House
Mamhilad
Mon
NP4 8RG

www.saronpublishers.co.uk
info@saronpublishers.co.uk
Follow us on Facebook and Twitter

ACKNOWLEDGEMENTS

The author is grateful to present and former residents of New Market Street for allowing him to see documents and deeds and for their willingness to spend time in recalling their knowledge of their property and former inhabitants: Claire Humphreys, Ceri Mowat, Fiona Powell, Dora Sale, C Southwell and Heather Taylor. Thanks are extended to Rosemary Evans for the loan of books, pamphlets and newspaper cuttings about Usk and some of its residents. Pat Sanderson kindly lent a copy of the book she and Deborah Wildgust have written relating the story of Pontypool and Usk Japanware. Huge thanks are due to Jon Prince for his dedication in taking the best possible photos of New Market Street, and for his design skills for the cover. Some of the photographs of Victorian and early 20th century Usk are from the collections of John Latham and Graham T Emmanuel, to whom thanks are extended, as they are to Godfrey Brangham about the history of his former home. He and the Treasurer of Usk Civic Society, Barry Morse, kindly read an early draft and their comments and advice greatly improved its contents and appearance. The help and experience of Penny Reeves in preparing it for printing was invaluable and the printing of it by Saron Publishers was magnificently efficient. The publication had been assured by grants from Usk Civic Society and the Roger Edwards Educational Trust, for which the author is most grateful.

Map of Usk taken from William Coxe's *Tour in Monmouthshire* 1800

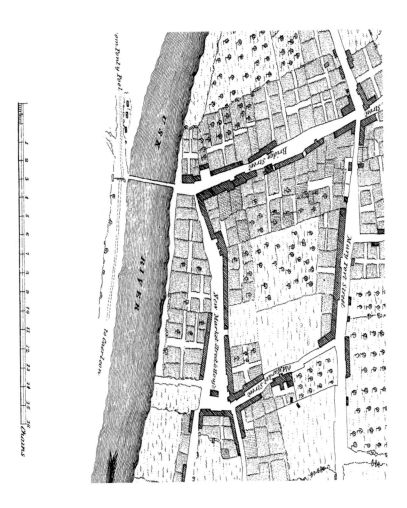

New Market Street: diagram showing property locations
(not to scale)
P = Plaque

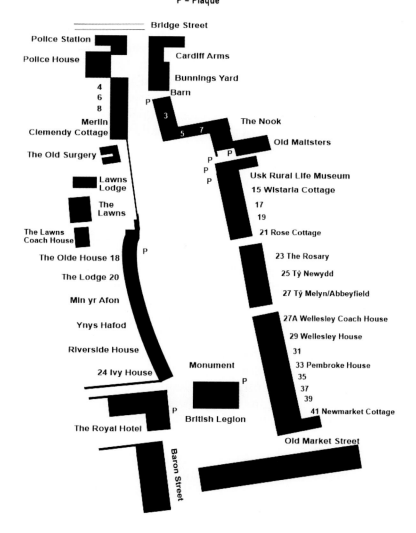

Introduction

New Market Street is regarded by many residents and tourists as one of the most attractive streets in Usk. It has a wide range of buildings and styles from the earliest - pre-16th century - through the Georgian and Victorian periods, with examples ranging from half-timbered to terraced and double-fronted residential homes. Aligned north to south, it is outside the limits of the ditches of the original Norman town and has developed over a period of five centuries. Many of the properties are listed as of architectural or historic importance under the Town & Country Planning Acts and the whole street is within a Conservation Area.

Although there are references to property sales and land transactions in the early 17th century, in deeds deposited in Gwent Archives, it proves difficult to identify their location. A list of burgage plotholders, tenants and rents in 1630 names eighteen burgage plots plus the market hall[1] but a list of 1634 names only nine.[2] This reduction seems typical of the economic fluctuations of Usk over the centuries as discussed by Paul Courtney.[3] The earliest overall illustration of the street appears in a map *(see earlier)*, published in July 1800 and contained in *An Historical Tour in Monmouthshire* by William Coxe. This shows the eastern frontages from Bridge Street southwards consisted of small cottages as far south as Old Market Street.

The western side has buildings only on the section south of No 18 (The Olde House) as far as River Lane. The absence of dwellings in this area could be attributed to its periodic flooding from the river before the flood banks were built.

---

[1] Bradney p 32

[2] JHC p 222

[3] PC p 109

In more recent times, a former resident of No 14 (now Clemendy Cottage) has childhood memories of the floods and of people canoeing down the street.[4]

The modest dwellings of the period before the 18th century have often been replaced by grander properties over the last two hundred years.

In the 19th century, at least 30 butchers worked in Usk and many held their 'shambles' on the pitched causeways each side of the street, under a dilapidated wooden roof. The last to leave was in the lean-to building (now a hairdressers) and once the barrel store[5] next to the Queen's Hotel, one of six ale houses in the street.

---

[4] JN

[5] AL p 36

New Market Street looking south with No 1 on the left before it was demolished to extend Bunning's Yard.

Description of individual properties with reference to the diagram locations

EAST SIDE

From Bridge Street southwards, the first property was a public house, formerly known as The Pelican, owned by Thomas Wigginton in 1846 and by Joseph Williams in 1851.[6] On redevelopment and expansion, it was renamed the Cardiff Arms and the landlord in 1901 was William Russell. **Bunning's Yard** was the site of the final factory producing Usk's Japanware. It was bought by Evan Jones in 1826 but the industry had been started in Pontypool in 1684. After a family dispute in the Allgood family, a group had moved to New Market Street in 1763. The first location was next to the George Inn where the works employed up to 20 workers. It was in decline when bought by Edwin Jones who moved to what is now known as Bunning's Yard. The gradual decline continued because of competition from cheaper Birmingham Japanware. By the time of Jones' death in 1860 and closure of the Usk business, there were only two brothers named Stockham working in the factory. The remains of the brick oven in which the wares were baked were demolished in about 1975, as was No 1 in New Market Street, adjoining The Cardiff Arms when Messrs Bunning built their easternmost storage shed.[7] The cottage where the Allgood family lived may have been the one to the south of the yard (No 3). Jones himself lived in a house on the site of Bunning's main shop front in Bridge Street *(but see the later section regarding Tŷ Newydd and Wellesley House)*.[8]

---

[6] JMB

[7] See photograph: JL

[8] UTT page 20; plaque

Nos 5 and **7** are identified by CADW as Georgian or with Georgian frontages.[9]

---

[9] UCPT page 131

The Nook *(above right)* and **The Old Maltsters** *(overleaf)* are regarded as two of the most important buildings in the town and almost certainly began as a single house. It was probably built and occupied as a town house by William ap Thomas, the royal steward of the lordship of Usk from 1431 until his death in 1445. (plaques). It has Tudor doorways and a first floor mullioned window. Indoors are three arched doorways and the screen end of a Tudor hall house. On the upper storey, there is a tiny 13th century window, carved from a single stone.[10] It is not known who had these properties built but they must have belonged to a wealthy man in 16th century Usk.

Richard Jones, the Usk maltster, lived here in 1774.[11]

---

[10] JMB

[11] JMB

By 1881, it was the home of Jane Blower, 72, who was listed as retired and seemed to be living on her own.

Usk Rural Life Museum at its northern elevation has a medieval mullioned window. Inside are the remains of pads on the tops of the front and back walls of the main room. These appear to have been the bases for an original arch-braced or even hammer-beamed roof. This building was a hall house, dating from the start of re-building after the 1402 attacks by Owain Glyndŵr, in which most of Usk was burned down. However, it is also possible that these are the remains of a hall house constructed before 1402 but so badly damaged by Glyndŵr's men that it had to be replaced by the house across the open way to the north, later becoming the barn of the maltsters living across the alleyway.[12]

The Museum opened here in 1981, having been founded as the Llanvapley Rural Crafts Preservation Society with its first exhibition in the local village hall in 1967. (three plaques).

---

[12] UCPT page 126–127

The eastern side of New Market Street south of the present Rural Life Museum (above). The eastern side of New Market Street, south of The Rosary (below).

Dates unknown but probably later than 1885 as Tŷ Newydd and Tŷ Melyn can be seen. Source: UCSC

No 11 was occupied in 1851 by William Stephens, a schoolteacher[13], with two children (1851 Census).

---

[13] DRL page 26

No 15 Wistaria Cottage was occupied by Walter Horsfield in 1895[14] and later in 1901 by Albert King, Usk Railway Station Master.[15] By 1911 William Weare, his wife, son, two grandsons and a boarder were in residence. A grocer's assistant by the name of Frank Nelmes was living separately at the address and was presumably linked somehow with Mr Nelmes who had the grocer's shop on the corner with Old Market Street *(see later)*. In the 1950s, it was the home and surgery of dentist William Humphrey (died 1968). The brass plate advertising his practice has been found and retained by the present householder.

Along with most of the properties in New Market Street, it was listed in May 1974 as a building of special architectural interest, under the Town and Country Planning Act 1971.

---

[14] KD 1895

[15] KD 1901

The White Lion Inn, now Nos 17 and 19, New Market Street

No 17 was an alehouse in 1813. Edmund Rees and David Williams are identified as cordwainers (an ancient term for shoemakers) in the Alehouse Recognizances of that date. In 1830 it was occupied by Isaac Williams and then by William Morgan in 1833. The 1841 census named it as the White Lion Inn, inhabited by another butcher Phillip Herbert, who lived there with his wife Rachel and three children. Two of the 18 Army servicemen who were living on New Market Street were lodging at the White Lion in 1841. A butcher, Isaac Williams (is this the same man who lived there in 1830?), owned it in 1846. In 1851 it was a public house – still called The White Lion - owned and by now inhabited by Benjamin Weare[16] and known as White Lion Cottage. It features in an undated photograph which clearly shows its inn sign, no front garden wall, horse

---

[16] DRL page 26

drawn carts and carriages in the street.[17] The Herberts were living elsewhere on New Market Street by 1861, together with John Weare (possibly Benjamin's son) who had married their daughter Anne.

By 1881, the White Lion was occupied by Jonathan Fricker, a 'gardener out of employment', whose (possible) brother James was resident at the Queen's Head Inn, further up New Market Street. By 1891, a 34-year-old widow called Amy Radford was now the publican, together with two children. By 1901, it seemed to have come into the hands of Thomas Parry.[18]

The White Lion on the left, looking south.
Source: GTE

No 19 was the home in 1861 of James Nurse, Blacksmith, with his wife Sarah, sister-in-law Mary Barlow and servant Samuel Higton.

---

[17] RE

[18] JMB

No 21, Rose Cottage, was, in 1835, Usk's first post office.[19] The Postmaster in 1841 was Henry Matthews, who lived there with his wife Ann and 8-year-old Maria, who may have been a granddaughter. Letters from London and Bristol arrived by horse-post every evening at 4.30pm and were despatched every morning at 6.30am. Those from Raglan came at 3pm and were sent at 9.30am.

By 1861, Rose Cottage was occupied by William Phillips, a retired farmer, who lived there with his wife, four children, his nephew and one servant.

In 1901, it was occupied by Lawrence Davies (aged 36), described in the Census as a 'Relieving Officer' and Registrar, with his housekeeper Susan Apsey (aged 52).

---

[19] UTT page 8

Ten years later, William Roberts, a law clerk, aged 34, lived here with his wife Florence, also 34, two children and a servant, Ethelwyn Meredith.

The cottage frontage has been raised by a box construction and the interior has two fine stone fireplaces. The upper floor has the only remnant portion of early wall painting in Usk.[20] This is reminiscent of that in the upper chamber of a house in Iron Acton in Gloucestershire of about 1550[21].

[20] UTT page 18

[21] UCPT page 125

No 23 - The Rosary - has a pleasing Georgian frontage in what may have been a Queen Anne house (1702-1714), enlarged from a small early 1600s property. Rear windows suggest the earlier period while the height may have increased considerably with gentrification and may have been the same originally as that of Rose Cottage next door.

Its best-known tenant was James Henry Clark, proprietor of Usk's newspaper, its historian and its last Portreeve. Clark later moved to the rather grand house in Bridge Street which eventually became the NatWest bank and is now 57 Bridge Street – a restaurant[22].

A previous owner suggested Rose Cottage and The Rosary were in one occupation and ownership. A conveyance of April 1904 refers to the sale of both and there is physical evidence in the interiors of a link between the two, since removed by interior renovation. A conveyance of 1920

---

[22] UTT page 18

refers to a separation of the two.[23] This might explain the existence of a right of way from the street to the back of The Rosary via the passageway at the side of Rose Cottage and to its rear and then to The Rosary itself.

No evidence has been found on the origin of its name. As it is next to Rose Cottage and the gardens produce a prolific display of roses, recent owners have conjectured that the name is more floral than religious.

In 1871 it was occupied by Mrs Margaret Roberts, aged 83, her daughter, also Margaret, a second daughter Mary Voyce and her husband Charles. They were not listed in the 1881 census but reappeared by 1891, though Mary seemed to have died, as Charles was living here with Miss Roberts. Only Margaret was still there in 1901[24], with a second cousin and a servant. The house had passed to Louisa Evans by 1911 who lived there on 'private means'.

A family by the names of Parrish was certainly living there during WWII, as EI Parrish spent much of the war as a POW.

---

[23] CS

[24] KD 1901

No 25 Tŷ Newydd *(above left, with Tŷ Melyn, right).*
Both the present Nos 25 and 27 were built in about 1885 by
Dr James Boulton, living next door, for his two daughters.
What occupied the site before 1885 isn't clear. At one time,
it was thought to be the first site of the Japanware works in
Usk which were established by a member of the Allgood
family after a dispute in the family in Pontypool.[25] *(See also
No 27A and No 29.)* Recent discoveries of old documents
at Wellesley House, however, suggest that the works were
there rather than at Tŷ Newydd, before being demolished
and the activity moved to Bunning's Yard. In 1911, it was
home to Alfred Watkins, a local solicitor, and his family.

---

[25] KD 1901

No 27 Tŷ Melyn *(see previous page)* is on the site of the George Inn. In 1813, Thomas Edwards and John Bowen Harvard, schoolmaster, were granted permission to run a 'common ale house'.[26] By 1830 the innkeeper was Joseph Carr and by 1835 John Williams. No one seemed to stay very long!

In 1841, five Army personnel were lodging at the George Inn, along with, among others, James Williams, a 'brightsmith', a worker in tin. The 1841 census is confusing in that it does not clearly differentiate between households. As James appeared to be living in the George Inn with his wife and four children, which seems unlikely, it may be this was a separate household, as by 1851 he and Margaret were definitely in their own house with the addition of two more children, though the eldest daughter Isabel is not mentioned. She would have been 17 by 1851 so may well be living elsewhere. By 1861, Margaret had become a schoolmistress, one daughter remained at home, now with her husband, and the two youngest children were also present. The 1871 census included James and Margaret, together with two grandsons, one of whom belonged to the daughter and son-in-law mentioned in the 1861 census, of whom there is now no trace. Indeed, James and Margaret did not appear in the 1881 census.

In 1843 Usk Female Benefit Society held their annual feast there, attended by 200 members, which says much about the size of the inn. In 1846, the inn passed into the ownership of James Williams, a brightsmith who lived in Old Market Street, who installed William Lewis, a labourer to run it.[27]

By 1861, Robert Breese was listed as living at the George Inn as a 'victualler and gardener'. He is interesting as the

---

[26] JMB

[27] DRL page 86

1841 census showed him, a 'publican', living somewhere on New Market Street, while the 1851 census listed him only as a 'seedsman and gardener', again with no identifiable address.

The inn featured in an indenture document of 1875 between James Boulton (Surgeon) and Emma Boatfield concerning settlement of land and property prior to their marriage, identifying the property and land owned by James Boulton and a reference to a blacksmith's shop.[28] This is confusing. Surgeon James' wife Catherine was alive in 1871. His son James was 29 and a civil engineer. So which James married Emma? There was another son, Donald, also a surgeon, who by 1871 was living on New Market Street with his wife Clara and daughters Catherine and Edith, plus Clara's mother, Catherine Gething, maybe a relative of Rachel Gething who was living at Ivy Cottage by 1901. By 1881 Donald was employing a live-in governess for the girls. Both girls were unmarried and living at home in 1901. Donald died before 1911 when Clara was listed as head of the household at Tŷ Melyn, with daughter Catherine and one servant.

---

[28] CM

No 27A - Wellesley Coach House and Wellesley House, No 29 *(above)* were originally one house, split in the late 1980s. The name and the style tend to date them as being in the very early 1800s, the Regency period. As in the case of other properties, it was almost certainly erected on the site of earlier small houses, such as the one immediately to the south which has a fine internal Tudor doorway. The old and new properties are linked to the Allgood family and to the manufacture in Usk of Japanware in the late 18th and through the 19th centuries

Japanware had been produced in Pontypool from the early 18th century, notably by the Allgood family. In 1761, Edward, a grandson of the founder, quarrelled with this family, left town and set up, with his brother, a rival establishment in Market Street in Usk near to the town hall. Both the Pontypool and Usk works were commercially highly successful and although sometimes in competition, at others they helped each other with orders.

By the late 1700s the works were run by Thomas Hughes - 'The Elman', a nephew of Edward Allgood - with members of the Stockham family. In the early 1800s, John Pyrke, a seller of tea, coffee and related goods (with shops in London), took over from Hughes. Pyrke expanded the business at his premises in New Market Street 'next to the George Inn'. This is now believed to be Wellesley House (ie the house and coach house) as the current owners have discovered some of John Pyrke's 200-year-old papers under the floorboards of their attic. Pyrke's proprietorship of the Usk Japanning works appears to have raised standards and he sold his wares to a wealthier clientele, including King Louis XVIII of France, the Duke of Beaufort and the Duke of Wellington. The latter had become famous when, as Arthur Wellesley, he led an army in India and later in Spain which expelled the French in the Peninsular war in the first decade of the 19th century. The connection between his name and that of the house seems more than coincidental.[29]

According to DRL in 1851, a surgeon, James Boulton,[30] practised medicine from No 29, where he lived with his first wife Catherine, three children and two servants. James was also surgeon to the newly-opened House of Correction[31] and had built Tŷ Newydd and Tŷ Melyn. By 1884, he was succeeded by his son, Donald Fludyer Boulton who was Medical Officer of Health to Pontypool Rural Sanitary Authority as well as surgeon to HM Prison Usk. By 1901, he had moved his surgery to Wellesley House and was a Member of the Royal College of Surgeons England.[32] His father died in September 1901.[33]

---

[29] Principally SCUJ

[30] DRL page 26

[31] JMB

[32] JMB

No 31 - This house has a fine internal Tudor doorway and is probably as early as any in this part of the street. Though enlarged at the rear by a single storey addition, and with a garage installed within its south side, it gives the impression of an early Georgian cottage and was named Brendon Cottage in the 19th and 20th centuries. In 1901 it was occupied by Mary Cherry[34] who, in 1911, was described as enjoying 'private means' at this address.

The garage conversion was undertaken by the father of the present owner–occupier, using an integral part formerly a scullery and thought to be where beer was brewed for sale on market days, as seems to have been the practice of many households (Source: DS).

---

[33] CM

[34] KD

No 33 Pembroke House and **No 35**. The site of these two large houses was occupied by a single cottage until 1851. It was the home of William Edwards, a tiler and plasterer, until his death in 1841, and then of William Taylor, a millwright, and Winifred, his wife. By 1851, the cottage was so dilapidated that the owners decided it should be demolished and the site partitioned so that two houses could be built, one for the heirs of William Edwards and the other for William Taylor. These two large houses are now Pembroke House and No 35.[35]

---

35 FP

Nos 37-39 show evidence on one of their frontages of a shop. The picture of the unveiling of the monument in New Market Street shows a sweet shop on this frontage.[36] There were references in 1851 to a private school, owned and run by Alice Dixon and her niece Mary Dixon, with five boarding pupils aged 8, 9 and 10, two of whom seem to be brothers, and a servant in this locality.[37] The 1861 census had no mention of this, though intriguingly one house, probably No 8 at the other end of the street, *(see later)* was occupied by a butcher Edmund Dixon, his wife Hannah, and daughter.

---

[36] JL

[37] DRL page 26

No 41 Newmarket Cottage was the home of one of Usk's [then] oldest inhabitants, Florence (Flossie) Gertrude Williams, who died in a nursing home in June 1975 aged 91. She was the last surviving child of Mr and Mrs Tom Williams, her father being a water bailiff in the Usk and Ebbw fishery district. The family was living on New Market Street, probably at Newmarket Cottage, by the 1891 census when Florence was 6.

In the 1911 Census, Tom and his wife Mary had two daughters still living at home - Rose and Florence, both dressmakers - and two lodgers, a postman, Herbert Stickler, and a chauffeur, Wilfred Jarvis.

Tom claimed to trace his ancestry back to the reign of William the Conqueror and his ancestors included the several times High Sheriff of Gloucestershire in the 15th and 16th centuries, whose son was martyred, burned at the stake, during the Reformation in 1531. Flossie was a remarkable singer, actress and a producer of amateur plays. She was an active member of the WI, and an ARP warden in WWII and was associated with the Red Cross and St John's Ambulance. When her local vicar dispensed with lady choristers, she transferred to Llanbadoc church where she was buried in 1975.[38]

Philanthropic Inn

Somewhere in this area of New Market Street once existed yet another pub, called The Philanthropic Inn. It has proved impossible to identify the exact location. In 1861, it was being run by Henry Jenkins, aged 31, a beer-house keeper, who lived there with his wife Hannah and little son, also Henry, aged 1. By 1871, the Jenkinses were still running the pub and had been joined by an older daughter, Ann, now 13, Henry, now 11, and five further children, Albert, Samuel, Arthur, Ellen and Benjamin. By 1881, Ann, Henry and Albert were no longer living there, and neither was Benjamin. The remaining three children had, however, been joined by Edgar, Agness, Florence, Edith and Beatrice. There was no trace of the family anywhere in the area in the 1891 census.

---

[38] Newspaper cuttings RE

Corner of New Market Street and Old Market Street. The space on this corner adjoining No 41 was once occupied by a grocer's shop – owned by Mr Nelmes - who vacated it to live opposite in his shop in Old Market Street. The photograph[39] *(above)* shows the property before it was subsequently used as a fish and chip shop which is said to have burned down, and the site was never re-occupied.[40]

---

[39] JL

[40] Recollections of RE and DS

*The southern end of New Market Street;
date unknown but the display of flags and
bunting suggests this may have been taken
shortly before the unveiling of the Memorial
in 1908. Source: UCSC*

WEST SIDE

The map reproduced earlier from William Coxe's *An Historical Tour in Monmouthshire* in 1800 shows there were no buildings in the length of the western side of New Market Street southwards from Bridge Street for approximately 120 yards (ie as far as The Olde House, Number 18). This means that all the properties northwards from No 18 were built in the 19th century or later.

Police station

In 1895, Edward Rowen (sergeant) and two constables occupied the station.[41] In 1901, William Sheddick (sergeant), with his wife Margaret and three children were in occupation. Two constables were also stationed there.[42]

---

[41] KD 1895

[42] KD 1901

Nos 4, 6 and 8. These three early Victorian cottages were occupied in 1851 by a labourer, a fisherman and a milliner.[43] In 1861 one house was occupied by Edmund Dixon, a butcher, his wife Hannah, and daughter. By 1871, Edmund had died and Hannah had taken over the business and was living with her daughter, son-in-law and five grandchildren. By 1881, she was managing the Queen's Head Inn, probably the unnamed home (Number 8?) in the earlier censuses. An undated photograph, looking southwards, *(see opposite page),* has a sign hanging on this group's frontage with the words 'The Queen's Head by James Fricker, licensed retailer of beer, porter and cider'.[44] By 1891, Edgar Thomas had taken over both butcher's and inn. By 1901, the landlord was John Price.[45] By 1911, the inn was in the hands of John Hobson.

---

[43] DRL – page 26

[44] RE

[45] JMB

The cottage named **Merlin** *(above right, with Clemendy Cottage, left)* was so called by the owner John Bright, who had earlier worked as a messenger for delivery of the *Monmouthshire Merlin* newspaper. On settling in Usk, he opened it as a public house with that name. By 1851, he had sold it to George Roberts, a painter and plumber, who also sold beer from the inn. The house name remains to this day.[46] In the 1861 census, it was called Merlin Inn, though there seems to be no evidence that it was actually an inn. By 1901, it was occupied by John Roberts, a retired house decorator, his wife, daughter and son Percy, listed as a 'retired compositor' and now Deputy Registrar of Births and Deaths.[47] Percy did well for himself as by 1911 he is listed as having 'private means'.

---

[46] DRL page 26

[47] KD 1901

Clemendy Cottage *(see previous page)* stands on the southern end of this terrace and in 1851, was occupied by Elizabeth Collins, a widowed school mistress.[48] Its name was given by a recent owner-occupier when he and his wife first bought it in 1979 and derives from the writings of Arthur Machen of Caerleon - *The Chronicle of Clemendy*. In 1879, it was the home of a prison officer named George Whiting who was responsible for the release of Josef Garcia after he had served his time in Usk Prison for burglary. Garcia went on to commit murders in Llangybi for which he was found guilty and hanged, (though there are doubts by modern historians about his guilt).[49]

[48] DRL page 26

[49] GB

The Old Surgery was built by WH Sweet for Dr Bird and Dr Horton for their general practice after WWII. The surgery had previously been held in Dr Bird's house - Riverside House - a little further along the street.[50] The practice later moved to its present building - James House - near the town's main car park.

[50] AL page 14

Lawns Lodge was built in the 1980s in the grounds of The Lawns by George Sweet, a local builder, for his residence.

The Lawns *(above).* This fine, large house is now divided into flats. It was probably built for the vicar of Usk, the Rev Thomas Addams-Williams, just before his marriage in November 1785. The building does not appear on Coxe's map of Usk and one source states that it was built in the early 19th century.[51] The Rev Thomas Addams-Williams was appointed vicar of Usk in April 1784 by his father, the patron of the living. It seems to have retained church links as by 1851, it housed a clergyman, Arthur Williams. In 1871, he was recorded as Vicar of Llanbadoc, living there with his sister Annabella, two nieces and a servant. By 1881, Arthur Williams was 72 years old and described in the census as a 'clergyman without care of souls'! Only one niece remained, with one servant. By 1901, Bernard Channer, a Colonel on the Indian Staff Corps, lived here,

---

[51] DRL page 26

along with his wife and a nine-year-old son, as well as a parlourmaid, housemaid and cook. It was still in private hands by 1911 when Robert Beasley and his wife Rebecca lived here with four servants. It gained notoriety in the late 1930s when, as a Gentleman's Club, it was raided several times unsuccessfully by the local police, until it was realised that a relation of one of the owners of The Lawns worked for the police and could warn of planned raids. A raid during her absence interrupted the out of hours drinking, gambling and other more dubious activities, with people fleeing in all directions. It was reported with relish in the local newspapers that some of them were wading across the river to the rear in various states of undress.[52] The subsequent trial evidence uncovered a series of warning bells that were operated from the bar but rang in the club bedrooms.[53]

Lawns Coach House is a conversion of the original coach house.

[52] UTT page 17

[53] AL

No 18 The Olde House is Usk's last surviving jetted, half-timbered house. Probably built before 1550, it has various styles, sometimes hidden from the road. The rear has a gable chimney and fireplace, stairs and a roof possibly containing upper crucks. The southern side wall, now the entrance passage, was probably timber-framed. The front section, a cross wing, is mainly half-timbered with stone lower portions. The four light mullioned and sunk chamfered windows on this wall should be of 1600-1625 and maybe replaced a diamond mullioned window which agrees better in date with the rest of the façade. Part of the northern portion is probably a parlour added in the 18th or 19th century.[54] Greatly altered over the centuries, it has some very fine woodwork, including a rounded, bar-stopped main beam, unusual but not unique in the area.[55]

---

[54] UCPT page 26; attributed to Peter Smith, the former secretary of the Royal Commission of Ancient and Historic Monuments, Wales

[55] UTT page 16

No 20 The Lodge were stables and coach house for Ynys Hafod, and are believed to have been built in 1827. They were converted to a house after WWII.[56]

---

[56] JL & CH

Min yr Afon was occupied in 1851 by one of the many professional fishermen of Usk who needed a licence to fish after 1854 when free fishing was abolished to general uproar. The house is attached to Ynys Hafod *(see page overleaf)* and was the servants' quarters until it became a detached house.[57]

---

[57] JL

Ynys Hafod - 'the summer dwelling on the water meadow' - originally faced the river and dates from the 16th century, when Roger Williams of Llangybi's great friend and secretary John Rumsey lived here, having inherited it from John Thomas, a family member.[58]

The owner at one time was Illtyd Nichol (1775-1871), the owner of much property in the street and probably the wealthiest man in town. From about 1562, it was the home of John Rumsey who was employed both as secretary to Roger Williams (by then of Llangybi Castle and Sheriff of the county), and as Master of a school in Usk. This predated the grammar school endowed by Roger Edwards in 1621 by 50 years or so. The Rumsey family continued in Ynys Hafod until 1749 when one of their daughters sold it for £110 to a clergyman/relative who lived in Bath. He sold it in the next year for £350, an astonishing profit for a local clergyman who later substantially increased his fortunes

---

[58] JMB

via two wealthy wives. In 1807, his stepdaughter Elinor Bond married Illtyd Nichol, then of The Ham in Glamorgan, who moved to join her at Ynys Hafod.[59]

In 1851, the household consisted of Illtyd Nichol (Elinor had recently died), son William, daughter Ellena and eight servants. Illtyd was recorded as a 'landed proprietor' but his name did not feature in the next census in Usk but he was found living at The Ham, near Cowbridge, where he originated. Subsequently he became a boarder in North Road, Bath where he died in 1871. [60]

His son was living in Ynys Hafod in 1861 as 'a gentleman', aged 41 with his wife, 'a lady', and eight servants still.

William became the centre of a town scandal when, later in the 1860s, he formed a relationship with Elizabeth Paine, (one of the eight servants listed in the 1861 census), and left the area to live with her and raise a family. His grave in Usk churchyard has the epitaph, 'I have blotted out as a thick cloud thy transgressions and as a cloud thy sins', which suggests the family found it hard to forgive him.[61]

By 1911 it was home to Samuel Hackett, a 'registered medical practitioner', his wife, two children, a nurse, cook, parlourmaid and a children's nurse.

By 1918, the family of Nicholl were back in residence, as they wrote to the Usk War Memorial Committee offering the life-size oil painting of the largest salmon ever caught in the Usk – 68$\frac{1}{2}$ lbs caught in 1782 – in order to help raise money for the proposed war memorial. The committee accepted the offer with thanks.[62]

---

[59] UTT page 16

[60] UTT page 16

[61] DRL page 26

[62] JMB

In WWII, the First Mons were stationed in the Town Hall and the officers were housed in Ynys Hafod. A sentry was stationed alongside the gap at the side of Ynys Hafod and would challenge anyone walking down that side of New Market Street. People would be told to walk on the opposite side of the road. Later in the war, land girls were also billeted here.

Riverside House, adjoining and south of Ynys Hafod, was once the site of a draper's and grocer's shop, pulled down in 1833.[63] A new house was built by Illtyd Nichol for his barrister friend Thomas Falconer in 1844 at a cost of £244. A double-fronted neoclassical façade, it is larger and architecturally more interesting than it may appear. Falconer was appointed the first judge for the district when the county court system was introduced in 1851.

According to one source,[64] he had left by March 1851 but the census record his residency until at least 1871, along with a brother, sister, two cousins, a governess and five servants. Interestingly, in 1871, a George Nicholl, a 'barrister not in practice and a magistrate', was visiting Riverside, as was Mary Nicholl who may have been George's wife, while also listed at the house were Frances (35) and Ellen (14) Nicholl. Was the governess for Ellen?

---

[63] AL page 17

[64] UTT page 16

By 1881, the now-retired Thomas Falconer had moved back to Walcot in Somerset, his birthplace, where he died in August 1882.

The house was subsequently occupied by the new prison chaplain, the Rev Kenyon Homfray, together with his mother Harriet and niece Eliza Smith. By 1891, it had become the home of Humphrey Humphreys JP[65], a retired Ceylon coffee planter, who in 1911 was still resident, though by now it was himself and his wife, plus a niece, cook, parlourmaid, sick nurse and a male nurse, which doesn't seem to have boded well for the health of either Humphrey or his wife Susannah, who were both 75.

---

[65] KD 1895 and 1901

Interesting chimney pots on Riverside, Min yr Afon and Ynys Hafod

No 24 Ivy House. No architectural details are available for this property but it appears to be 18th century.[66] Edward Waters, one of Usk's many tailors, lived here from 1834 until at least 1871.[67] In the 1891 census, it is home to William Whitehead, his wife, three children and a servant. William was a Sergeant Major Inspector to the Yeomanry Royal Gloster Hussars. In 1901, it was home to Mrs Rachel Gething, a widow,[68] 64 years old, living on her 'own means' with a 21-year-old servant Annie Jenkins. By 1911 it had become a boarding house, though seemed to only have had one resident, apart from the owner.

---

[66] UTT page 15

[67] JMB

[68] KD 1901

Between Ivy House and the Royal Hotel is **River Lane**, up which water was brought for the early fire engine and down which fire pumps were tested in WWII.

The Royal Hotel has two elegant bowed windows and was built by John Stephens, a timber merchant, as his home in about 1835. He still owned it in 1846 when it was known as the Royal Oak.[69] It was the first home of Edward John Trelawny (1792–1881), friend of Byron and Shelley, ex-pirate, incorrigible womaniser, traveller, romantic poet and author. He fought alongside Byron for Greek independence from the Turks and was with Byron and Shelley in Italy when the latter drowned. He organised Shelley's cremation in 1822 with Byron and Leigh Hunt, on the beach at Viareggio where the body had been washed up. He later arranged for the ashes to be buried in Rome's Protestant Cemetery, alongside those of Keats. His own were to be buried there sixty years later.

Many of the large cedar trees in and around Usk and Llanbadoc have grown from seeds that Trelawny brought back from the cemetery in Rome.

---

[69] JMB

He and his second (maybe third) wife moved to New Market Street in 1841 and lived in the house while he had built the house now called Twyn Bell (which he called The Cot or more appropriately The Prospect) on the hillside of the River Usk above Llanbadoc Church. The growing family lived there for some years before moving further uphill to the larger Cefn Ila House (since burned down). They were visited at one of their houses by the authoress of *Frankenstein* - Mary Shelley. Trelawny left Cefn Ila House in 1858 when he returned to London with yet another conquest, the young Miss B...., still untraced. He had brought her to the house and installed her as his mistress, an arrangement which caused his wife to leave him for Italy. Before then, the whole family had been a source of fascination to the locals, with their nude bathing in the river, their atheism and their 'back to nature' ways. Trelawny was a friend of the local historian, publisher and thrusting town official, James Henry Clark, then of Buxton House in Old Market Street. He helped Clark and his friends in their tree- and shrub-planting scheme on the Conigar Walk and elsewhere, and entertained Clark and others with his tales of adventures and poets.[70]

From 1851 to 1871, John Morgan was the landlord, succeeded by John Thomas. Between 1881 and 1891, The Royal, as it was now called,[71] was taken over by Richard Coleman, with his wife Eliza, a daughter and friend (both aged 19), a servant and a lodger William McLean, described as 'living on his own means'. Coleman does not seem to have lasted there long as by 1901, it was occupied by David John Davies with Tom Jones, coach builder and wheelwright, in buildings at the rear[72] as described below.

---

[70] UTT pages 14 and 15

[71] JMB

[72] KD 1901

By 1911 Tom Jones seemed to be also running the hotel. Local legend recalls that Tom Jones, who also ran the undertakers' business from the rear buildings, promised a free funeral to anyone who died when drinking at the Royal Hotel!

At the rear of The Royal Hotel, the large buildings and yard were, according to a copy of the parish magazine *The Ensign* of January 1949, occupied and used by Messrs T Jones (undertakers). They offered 'supreme funeral services, coffins manufactured on site together with motor-body building, wheelwrights and sawing, planing and moulding mills'. In June 1975, all the premises - a licensed house containing twelve main rooms, stores, garages, extensive cellars and the adjoining business and industrial premises - were auctioned after the death of Mr T Jones Jr. They were sold for £23,000 to Dr Russell Rees of Caerleon.[73]

---

[73] Magazine and press cuttings RE

The Old Town Hall, Market Hall and now **The Royal British Legion** stands as a detached building at the southern end at New Market Street.

According to Bradney,[74] the original market place was what is now called the Twyn (tump) where there may have been an earth mound, which gave its name to the square. This was subject to a conveyance dated 31st December 1459. A century later, it would seem to have moved to its present locality. On 14th July 1598, Henry, Earl of Pembroke, conveyed to the Portreeve, bailiffs and burgesses and his tenants in Usk a piece of waste land and a house to be built thereon, in the lower part of New Market Street, for holding a weekly market for ever, reserving a rent of one shilling per annum. This confirms that basically the whole of New Market Street and the adjoining end of Old Market Street had by then been built up as a suburb outside the limits of the obsolete Norman town ditch.

---

[74] Page 12

In this hall, the burgesses met and various courts and functions were held. It received at least two visits from King Charles I. The first was the occasion when he was seeking to raise the illegal tax known as Ship Money before he declared war on Parliament. The second was during the latter part of the first Civil War when he was trying to whip up support from a war-weary population.

The building has been re-designed and re-built on several occasions, including the closure of the arcades as being too draughty for stalls. Years of neglect took its toll and by the mid 18th century, the Market Hall had become too ruinous. The new Market House/Town Hall was completed by 1777.[75]

In 1814, the Quarter Sessions ordered the Clerk of the Peace to erect 'rooms adjoining the Town Hall in Usk' to provide 'places of detention'. The clock was also to be moved to the front of the new building, ie facing New Market Street.[76]

In the 1841 census, it was inhabited solely by six soldiers, out of the 18 who were lodging in the street. By 1859, the roof and ceiling of the Court had been raised by 10 feet and the basement had become apartments and cells for prisoners. A Muniment Room was added, a gallery, circular windows in the top storey and the roof reslated. This was probably when the arches on one side of the market hall were filled in to keep out the weather.

The lower storey became the first County police headquarters with its one cell, while the extension into New Market Street became the town fire station.

In WWII, the firemen had to sleep in the big room of the Town Hall so they were on the spot if the siren sounded.

---

[75] JMB

[76] JMB

Also billeted there were the men of the First Mons. A Home Guard trench once existed between here and Maryport Street.[77]

The construction of a police station at the junction at New Market and Bridge Street and of a new fire station on the Monmouth Road allowed new uses for the building, currently the Usk branch of The British Legion with rooms for entertainment and meetings.

---

[77] JMB

Monuments

In the centre of the street, north of The British Legion, is a monument inscribed: 'Erected by the inhabitants of Usk and District to the memory of Gunner John Williams (Royal Field Artillery), Private Thomas Bayliss, Private William Morgan (South Wales Borderers), Trooper Osmond H Haggett (Bethune's Mtd Infantry), who fell in the South African War 1899-1901, unveiled by James Henry Clark, the last Portreeve and now the oldest inhabitant; 11th January, 1908'.[78] James was 90 years old.

---

[78] See photograph JL

Unveiling on 11th January 1908 of the monument to the men killed in the Boer War.
Source: JL

Sources

AL: Anne Morgan: *A Portrait of Usk*

Bradney (William): *A History in Monmouthshire in three volumes*

CH: Claire Humphreys

CM: Ceri Mowat

Coxe, William: *An Historical Tour of Monmouthshire*

CS: C Southwell

DRL: David R Lewis *Early Victorian Usk 1982*

DS: Dora Sales

FP: Fiona Powell

GB: Godfrey Brangham

GTE: Graham T Emmanuel

HT: Heather Taylor

KD: *Kelly's Directory 1901*

JHC: James Henry Clark: *Usk Past and Present*

JL: John Latham

JMB: Janet Barrow: *From Dawn Till Dusk* and *Usk at War*

JN: Jacquelyn Nel (née Hawkins)

PC: Paul Courtney: *Report on the excavations at Usk 1965-1976: medieval and later Usk*

RE: Rosemary Evans

SC and UJ: Pat Sanderson and Deborah Wildgust and others: *The Story of Pontypool and Usk Japanware*: 2008

UCPT: *Usk Castle Priory and Town*: edited by Knight and Johnson

UCSC: Usk Civic Society collection of photographs

UTT: *Usk Town Trail*: Usk Civic Society 2010

About the Author

John Barrow was born in Birmingham in 1932. After primary and grammar school there, and two years of National Service, he studied for an Honours degree in Geography at Birmingham University. After graduation, he was appointed as a junior research assistant in the Cheshire County Council Town & Country Planning Department. During the three years there, he gained a special diploma in Town Planning from Manchester University and membership of the Town Planning Institute. He served on the staff of three county councils until he retired from Oxfordshire as Director of Planning & Property Services. He and his wife Janet (Jan) moved to Llanbadoc and lived in a cottage at Lower Prescoed, for over twenty years. In the first five years, he served as a local plans inspector in the Department of the Environment. Subsequently he became Chairman of Llanbadoc Community Council, then Secretary and Chairman of Usk Civic Society in which time many of the blue wall plaques and multi-coloured pavement plaques were installed in Usk. Jan wrote and published three books on local history. They moved into Usk about 10 years ago, where sadly Jan died in 2014.

About the Publishers

Saron Publishers has been in existence for about fourteen years, producing niche magazines. Our first venture into books took place in 2016 when we published *The Meanderings of Bing* by Tim Harnden-Taylor. Further publications include *Minstrel Magic,* by Eleanor Pritchard, George Mitchell's biography, *Penthusiasm,* a collection of short stories and poems from Penthusiasts, a writing group based in the beautiful town of Usk, and *Frank,* a gentle novel about loss, by Julie Hamill, followed in 2019 but its sequel *Jackie.*

2019 also saw the publication, among others, of Kevin Moore's second book, *Real Murder Investigations – An Insider's View,* which delves in more detail into some cases mentioned in his previous book, *My Way.*

Darcy Drummond's third novel, *High Manor,* following the successful *Summer Season* and *Water of Life,* is due out in late 2020.

Join our mailing list at info@ saronpublishers.co.uk. We promise no spam ever.

Visit our website saronpublishers.co.uk to keep up to date and to read reviews of what we've been reading and enjoying. You can also enjoy the occasional offer of a free Bing chapter.

Follow us on Facebook @saronpublishing.

Follow us on Twitter @saronpublishers.